2 -

IT'S A JAGUAR!

by Tessa Kenan

BUMBA BOOKS™

LERNER PUBLICATIONS ◆ MINNEAPOLIS

Note to Educators:

Throughout this book, you'll find critical thinking questions. These can be used to engage young readers in thinking critically about the topic and in using the text and photos to do so.

Lerner Publications Company
A division of Lerner Publishing Group, Inc.
241 First Avenue North
Minneapolis, MN 55401 USA

For reading levels and more information, look up this title at www.lernerbooks.com.

Library of Congress Cataloging-in-Publication Data

Names: Kenan, Tessa, author.
Title: It's a jaguar! / by Tessa Kenan.
Other titles: It is a jaguar!
Description: Minneapolis : Lerner Publications, [2017] | Series: Bumba books. Rain forest animals | Audience: Age 4–8. | Audience: K to grade 3. | Includes bibliographical references and index.
Identifiers: LCCN 2016021985 (print) | LCCN 2016026867 (ebook) | ISBN 9781512425710 (lb : alk. paper) | ISBN 9781512429343 (pb : alk. paper) | ISBN 9781512427608 (eb pdf)
Subjects: LCSH: Jaguar—Juvenile literature. | Rain forest animals—Juvenile literature.
Classification: LCC QL737.C23 K458 2017 (print) | LCC QL737.C23 (ebook) | DDC 599.75/5—dc23

LC record available at https://lccn.loc.gov/2016021985

Manufactured in the United States of America
1 – VP – 12/31/16

Expand learning beyond the printed book. Download free, complementary educational resources for this book from our website, www.lernerresource.com.

Table of Contents

Spotted Cats 4

Parts of a Jaguar 22

Picture Glossary 23

Index 24

Read More 24

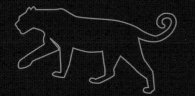

Spotted Cats

Jaguars are big cats.

They are the biggest cats

in South America.

Many jaguars live in rain forests.

Jaguars have tan or yellow fur.

Their fur has black spots.

Jaguars have long tails.

They have strong jaws too.

How might strong jaws help a jaguar?

Jaguars walk on
four paws.

Their paws have claws.

Jaguars use their claws
when they hunt.

Jaguars hunt mostly on the ground.

They chase any animals they find.

Sometimes jaguars hunt from

trees too.

Jaguars pounce on animals

from above.

Jaguars are

good swimmers.

They swim in rivers.

They catch fish and

crocodiles to eat.

Mother jaguars have one to four babies at a time. Jaguar babies are called cubs.

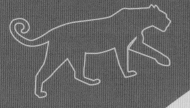

The cubs are blind at first.

They cannot live without

their mother.

The mother protects her cubs.

Why do you think mother jaguars protect their cubs?

The cubs leave their home

after two years.

They have learned to

hunt from their mother.

Adult jaguars live alone.

They protect their territory.

Other jaguars know to stay away.

How do you think other jaguars know to stay away?

Parts of a Jaguar

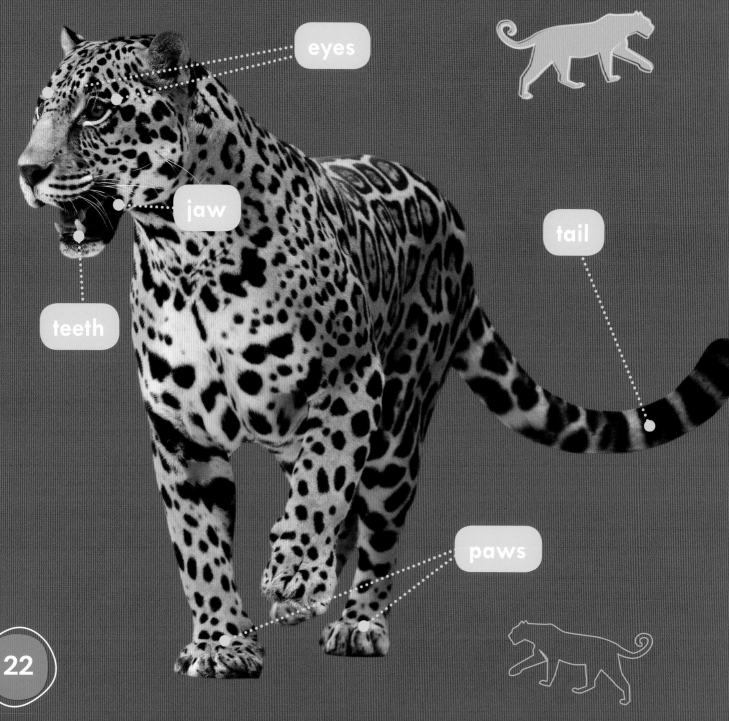

eyes

jaw

teeth

tail

paws

Picture Glossary

cubs

young jaguars

pounce

to jump forward and grab something suddenly

rain forests

thick, tropical forests where lots of rain falls

territory

a large area of land that an animal lives in and protects

23

Index

claws, 8

cubs, 15–16, 19

fur, 7

hunting, 8, 11, 19

jaws, 7

paws, 8

rain forests, 4

South America, 4

swimming, 12

tails, 7

territory, 20

Read More

Archer, Claire. *Jaguars.* Minneapolis: Abdo Kids, 2015.

Arnold, Quinn M. *Jaguars.* Mankato, MN: Creative Education, 2016.

Kenan, Tessa. *It's a Chameleon!* Minneapolis: Lerner Publications, 2017.

Photo Credits